Accounting Basics For Success In Business And In Life

SADANAND PUJARI

Published by SADANAND PUJARI, 2023.

Table of Contents

Copyright

Accounting Basics For Success In Business And In Life

First Edition: Dec 2023

Book Design by **SADANAND PUJARI**

About

Has Accounting always sounded like a foreign language to you?

Do Financial Statements add so much confusion to your life that you secretly avoid them?

If you are struggling to understand 'the numbers' as they say and have answered YES to ANY of these questions - You've come to the right place.

Apart from any of the humor - more importantly - This Book WILL give you a Good rundown into the world of Accounts - something which I believe will help you and your business in many ways throughout your lifetime.

Introduction

In this chapter we will take a look at what will be covered in accounting for corporations. We're currently in the Overview chapter of the Book as we scroll down through the Overview chapter of the Book.

We are now in the Book content chapter of the Book the Book content will be laid out by the chapter headers the chapter headers giving us an idea of what will be included as we go through the chapter headers you can see that there will not be a uniform or the same amount of material per chapter but the chapter headers will give us an idea what will be covered in each chapter. There will be some uniformity however to the type of material that will be included from chapter to chapter. That includes Of course instructional chapters as well as PTF files, pedia files that can be downloaded, pedia files that can be used as reference pedia files that can be worked with and worked on off line without the use of the internet connection.

We will also typically have Excel files Excel files that can be downloaded Excel files that can be worked along with the instructional chapters that will be with them so we can work through those in a step by step format the excel files typically have two tabs to them at least one tab will have the answer to it. And so you can see exactly what is happening with it. And then the other tab will give a pre-formatted worksheet that will be able to work through the problem along with instructional chapters. We will also typically have discussion questions and discussion questions will be open ended questions that you can go through and test the material.

We typically have multiple choice questions that you can work through as well and the multiple choice questions will be in chapter format but they'll go over multiple choice questions and test taking skills for them. We typically have a comic break which is only a couple of seconds long just to give a quick comic as we go through. This information will now go through the chapters by topic just to give an idea of what will be covered. The introduction will cover this as well as an introduction to the corporation form of entity discussing its characteristics and really why we would want to have a corporate form of entity as opposed to other types of industries or other types of entities such as partnership or sole proprietor. Then we have the issue of common stock we're going to get down to the transactions.

Now the common stock being issued is similar to a partner or a sole proprietor investing in the partnership that's typically going to be the initial investment that happens and what happens periodically as the corporation wants to grow. They're going to ask for money from owners from stockholders that will be the issuance of stock. Doesn't happen quite as often as we would think. When we look at the stock market because obviously we're trading stock all the time with the stock market but most of that stock trades aren't issued from the company. The company is going to be the initial issue and then some issues after that.

Hopefully then after that point the company will be earning revenue and giving money to the owner in the form of dividends. We'll talk about the transaction for the issuance of stock both in terms of the transaction issue and for cash or non-cash such as equipment. We'll have the concept of cash dividends stock dividends. These are going to be the idea of what a dividend will compare and contrast the dividend to what is similar in other types of entities like a sole proprietorship or partnership which will be drawn. What's the difference between draws and dividends?

We'll discuss that and how to record the dividends, it being a bit more of a bureaucratic process for a corporation than possibly it would be for a partnership or sole proprietor to record draws. Well take a look at preferred stock comparing and contrasting what is preferred stock as compared to common stock. We'll look at treasury stock once again discussing what is Treasuries doc as compared to preferred stock or a common stock. We'll talk about how to record treasury stock and why the company might have treasury and preferred stock. We'll look at the statement of stockholders equity and the statement of retained earnings. Those are going to be the statements we focus on because those will be the ones that will differ from other business entity types meaning the main things that differ for a corporation are going to be the equity chapter.

The format of ownership, the type of ownership that is through stock stockholders being the owners as opposed to partners or sole proprietors for a partnership or sole proprietorship, then we're going to have the closing process once again focusing on what differs within the closing process. So we will look at what will be the same as well we'll go through the entire closing process a four step closing process but really it's the component that is closed out to the equity chapter to retained earnings in this case which will differ from the closing process of other entity types like partnership or sole proprietor which causes out to not retained earnings but capital accounts. They will talk about earnings per share. What it is, how to calculate it.

Why would we calculate how it can be used and then we'll have a comprehensive problem. The comprehensive problem designed to take a step back not look so much at the things that differ but look at the things that are the same. Note the things that are going to differ and note you know what the proportion is in terms of daily transactions that will be the same and the things that will differ. Meaning most business transactions will be much the same from different entity types. The things that will differ will often be the things we're focusing on in this Book. It's always good to take a step back and look at the full perspective.

This comprehensive problem may change over time we may update the comprehensive problem but the point here is to really go through the accounting cycle again and just think as you go through the accounting cycle what how significant or how often do these things that we're learning going to play in to that normal process the normal day to day increase as we go through the entering of journal entries for the normal types of transactions. Posting them to the general ledger creating the trial balance, doing the adjusting entry process created in the financial statements and then having the closing process.

Corporation Introduction

In this chapter we will take a look at the corporate form of business organization as we go through the corporate form. We want to be able to compare and contrast this and think in your mind. What is different here between the corporation and other types of business entities like a partnership like a sole proprietor. So when we take a look at any of these one types of entities it's useful for us to make that comparison and think about what the corporation is. How is the corporation different and how is it similar to other business entity formats?

Note that as we go through the corporations we will be focusing on those areas that are different and that could lead us to start to think that all business entities are going to be very different in the way we record transactions and the way they interact. But really they're not. Most of the transactions will be much the same. We as accountants will always have the corporations separate from us. We'll record the double entry accounting system and we'll still be in balance. All of that will remain the same. Where we focus on these different types of entities will be the areas where they differ. For corporations as with all entities where they differ most is the format of ownership the equity chapter.

In this case stockholders equity for a corporation. So corporate overview what are going to be some differences between the corporation and roomer. We are focusing on those differences. One is that it's going to be a separate legal entity and that kind of leads to some of the other differences. That's the major breakthrough of a corporation when it was kind of invented. The idea of the corporation was behind the fact that it is a separate legal entity now from a bookkeeping perspective. That's not a whole lot different from how we treat books all the time. If we are a sole proprietor even if we file a Schedule C tax return on our normal individual income taxes for our business as a sole proprietor we still look at our business as a separate legal and not a legal and as a separate entity.

In order for us to judge how the company is doing in other words we want to see our revenue and expenses from our business side separate from our personal revenue expenses. We want to measure our performance from a business perspective different from our performance from a personal perspective that the objectives are different business. We're looking to get revenue from the personal side we're looking to live well. So those are two different objectives. We always keep the book keeping separate but the corporation is a separate legal entity meaning that the actual legal component of it has given it certain rights which typically are only given to individuals such as the right to own property and the responsibility to do things such as pay taxes some of the major benefits of being a separate legal entity.

Is that because it actually owns property in of itself that entity does then when you sue a corporation or if they have any liability problems then you could be really going after that corporate entity and not necessarily the owners of the corporate entities. So it provides some liability protection. So it's going to have rights and privileges in of itself. Again giving the corporate entity certain rights and privileges to own property and therefore their responsibilities along with those rights and privileges or corporation could either be privately held or publicly held.

When we think about corporations we typically think about big corporations like Apple or Google and we typically think about publicly held corporations but privately held that would basically mean that the stock is not being traded on a public stock exchange. So in other words if it's not traded on a public stock exchange you're not going to be able to go and basically just buy and sell the public shares through the public stock exchange is going to be privately held publicly traded companies means that basically we can sell through a public exchange the public exchange will typically allow for the public to purchase the stock and have a lot of potential therefore to raise capital capital investment through the sale of stock.

Corporate characteristics include the separate legal entity and note that's going to be the main div or a big difference between a corporation and a sole proprietor or a partnership. We also have the limited liability which kind of stems from the separate legal entity because there is a separate legal entity the shareholders are going to have limited liability and that's a huge benefit because it allows us as even small investors to buy something like a mutual fund or something like that have an equity interest in a corporation but not have to worry so much that if the corporation goes under if they do something bad if they if they get sued or something like that then the court we might lose our investment. But they shouldn't therefore be able to come after our house or personal assets and that's a huge benefit that allows for investment into something like corporations and allows for business to get the capital needed to thrive.

We have transferable ownership and huge benefits as well. So we know that especially for a publicly held stock that they are going to be traded on the Stock Exchange. So when we see purchases of something like an apple or a Google type of stock you're not typically buying those stocks from the corporation. They typically have an initial stock offering and could issue stocks at a later point. But the stock being traded all the time is simply stock that's being traded from trader to Trader. And the beauty of the stock then is that the shares are all the same. So if one shares just like selling tokens or something like that that all have the same value the value will change over time as people perceive the value of the company to change. But all the stock theoretically should be the same in terms of units of the corporation and therefore all have the same value that's being traded. So that means that that allows that transfer ability something that we don't have in something like a partnership as easily.

Note that if we're in a partnership and you want to add a new partner or sell your partnership interest you will typically need that the go ahead from the other two partners. And it's a complex transaction to do that because you have to figure out how much of the interest you're going to sell and what the value of it is for the corporation because all the stocks are the same then that transaction to buy and sell the corporate stocks becomes a much easier thing to do. We have continued life again stemming from the separate legal entity concept. If you are a partnership or a sole proprietor then you're really not separate legally from your business again from a bookkeeping standpoint you are but because we're going to account for the books separately as if you are separate but you're not really separate in terms of a legal sense.

And that means that when someone dies or something happens or you know if someone quits the partner quits or something like that that basically ends the partnership and then needs to be reformed for a corporation. That's not the case if that if any person in the seat in the corporation dies whether it be the CEO the founder then the corporation lives on because the corporation has been given certain characteristics including a life you know basically that the ability to claim assets and whatnot to have those characteristics that typically individuals have and those characteristics can continue beyond any single individual. No. No mutual agency of stockholders.

Now this is really referring to a problem with our partnership which is a mutual agency problem meaning. We typically think of it as a problem meaning if two people get into a partnership or more people go into a partnership then all the partners can make contractual agreements and bind the other partners in an agency issue, meaning that the partnership then is responsible for the duties of whatever contract was agreed upon. And so one partner can make all the other partners basically responsible for that.

The reason it's not there for a corporation even though we may have far more owners of a corporation in terms of stockholders is that the stockholders cannot make you know what a normal does. Usually the stockholders are a step removed from the decision making process meaning the stockholders will then vote but they are not going to vote on day to day decisions. They're not going to make contract agreements typically they typically will vote for the board of directors who will then hire management then making the decisions. So that's going to be a few steps removed from a partnership type of situation.

Again there's pros and cons to that format. But you don't have the same type of agency problem as you do with a partnership ability to accumulate capital. This is one of the huge benefits of a corporation if you are a sole proprietor or a partnership and you have an idea and you want to implement this idea then it might be more difficult to raise the money for it because your. You'd have to get a loan for it which may be difficult to do to get equity interest. You'd have to get another partner to have the equity interest which is possible but when you have the ability to share to sell stocks and that becomes a lot easier to sell stocks to others to potential investors to get that equity interest and there are a lot more.

So a lot more enticing to an investor for a corporate stock because of the liability protection. So if I'm going to invest in other words into a general partnership, I'm worried about what happens if the partnership does something not very smart and they get sued or something and then I have my personal resources, my personal assets that could be taken or could be exposed to some liability through investing into that partnership. Whereas if we invest into a corporation we should have that corporate shield. We shouldn't be personally liable. We should all be able to lose up to our investment. So that's a huge benefit to raising capital problems including the fact that there's going to be more regulations involved with a corporation. To set up a corporation is typically more costly.

And maintaining a corporation is typically more costly. The other big problem is going to be that there is double taxation generally meaning a corporation is a normal corporation because once again it's a separate legal entity that is responsible for doing things that a normal person would do. Paying taxes being one of them. So they're going to have to pay taxes and then the corporation when it distributes those taxes to the owners in the form of dividends that dividends are taxable. So now we've got the corporation paying tax and then when they distribute to the owner the owner typically will pay tax whereas if you're a sole proprietor then you have a separate business but it really just flows through to the form 10 10:40 and the owner pays taxes on the individual level.

So that changes I mean that you know that that double taxation kind of changes whether or not how taxable those dividends will be could change as the laws change. But typically when you're going to get taxed on the corporate level and then the divisions get taxed on the. If you're a sole proprietor or partnership we call them draws you draw out the money from the partnership and because it's a flow through entity then we're just going to tax all of the income and the draws will not be taxed at a separate level. So that's going to be a huge downfall. You can also think that there is.

We talked about the mut. agency being a benefit that it doesn't have that problem that a partnership could have but the corporate structure is a lot more structured. So. So there could be issues with the corporate structure that the owners are a step removed oftentimes from the decision making process. And that could lead to its own kind of agency problems in terms of management agency problems when they're making their decisions about the well-being of the company because management Of course is there as an agent in order to represent the owners who are the are the stockholders the stockholders who basically voted in the board of directors to decide on management because of that step removal.

Management may have incentives as an agent to act in ways that are more personally beneficial rather than beneficial for the stockholders. So we can do the same kind of comparison with business entities just to keep in mind that relative comparison is a quick comparison between the different types of entities like a sole proprietor partnership LLP LLC corporation and corporation. So clearly we are here now. We're looking at the corporation and we're saying what's the difference between that between a proprietor and a partnership and then remember these three are kind of like hybrids of the two we're trying to get the best of both worlds. And if you look at the extremes here I just want to note that these two typically have the problem of more liability problems whereas the corporation being a separate legal entity has the benefit of liability protection.

On the other hand the corporation has the problem of double taxation because they're a separate legal entity and need to be taxed at the corporate level whereas the sole proprietor and partnership don't have the double taxation because there is a flow through entity and then these three are attempts to be hybrids. So attempts to have the best of both worlds attempts to have liability protection while still being able to have that light that's not being taxed on a devil taxation. So this is a limited liability partnership, a limited liability company. As a corporation. OK so a legal entity the proprietorship is not a separate legal entity.

Again we have the books kept kind of in a separate way but the proprietorship itself is not a separate legal entity. Neither is the partnership. Neither is the limited liability partner the limited liability company. On the other hand this hybrid method is going to be the separate legal entity as is the S-Corp and Of course the corporation is the separate legal entity. So then if we talk about the limited liability which is kind of an extension of the legal entity meaning the proprietorship because it's not a separate legal entity does not have the benefit of a limited liability meaning they are the personal liabilities of the owners or are exposed to any kind of problems any kind of lawsuit or something like that.

Same for the partnership. They don't have that benefit of a limited liability, the limited liability partner only the partner that is not engaged, a limited partner that's not engaged in the day to day operations. They have a benefit. And so that could be this format could be really beneficial if we have a good idea. But we need to get capital and we want to get an investor that has limited liability whereas we are just a normal partner so we get the benefits of being a partnership of which include things like them we get up flexibility with our arrangements and our profit sharing and we get the investment of the limited partner who is not exposed to the liability protection and therefore more likely to invest a limited liability company does have the benefit of a limited liability as does an S-Corp as it does Of course a corporation. Then we've got the business tax.

Are they going to be taxed at the business level? A sole proprietor. No. And this is going to be a benefit of a sole proprietor Why. Because if you're taxed on the business level typically you'll have double taxation because you'll be taxed at the business level and then you'll be taxed at the distribution level on the proprietor. You're taxed just as the business is taxed, net income taxed on the 10 40 distributions in the form of draws then are not going to be taxed again. Same with the partnership not taxed at the partnership level taxed at the partners level on their individual 10:40. The LLP again not is treated like a partnership not taxed on the business level but on the individuals the LLC limited liability company still taxed on the individual level. That's the benefit we're trying to get that liability protection by being a company type but still have that flow through process.

Taxed on the individual 10 forties and therefore not have double taxation. Same for an S Corporation this is more towards a corporation. But still we have that flow through a process that the tax is not going to be imposed on the corporate side could change for states by the way but for the federal tax but. And then and then it's going to be taxing the individuals 10:4 the corporation will be taxed on the corporate level. And that's the problem because once it's taxed on the corporate level it will most likely or oftentimes be taxed at distribution as well in the form of dividends. Meaning we'll have a double tax.

Can we have just one owner clearly proprietorship could a partnership cannot. If you are sober, if your partnership by definition you have two or more people, two or more individuals or organizations or something involved in it, the low P cannot be a partnership. The LLC generally you can and that seems like a contradiction. So there's a sole owner L-L see possible. And that you could know the laws could change from state to state in terms of that. The S-Corp you can own, so note that you can have one individual in other words owning the entire You could incorporate and own all the stock of a corporation or an S corporation. OK so if you take a look at the hierarchy for a corporation it's similar to that of a government. So if you look in a democracy you think of we the people or the people are supposed to you know be the ultimate owners of the country. And how do we exercise our ownership's while we vote?

We vote for representatives and then the representatives are going to hire people in order to do what needs to be done or whatnot so that the corporations form as much of the same meaning the owners are called stockholders. What's the major benefit of being a stockholder? You get to vote for like the decision makers you know you get the board of directors and the board of directors major goal is to represent the stockholders and therefore you know do the best thing they can for the business. Hire management. And then the management will be there in order to act as agents of the stockholders and they will hire other employees in order to run the business.

Similar structure. We're going to be a step removed then as the owners. So again if it's a closely held corporation then you're going to have more influence if you're someone that owns a few stocks of a publicly traded corporation than you're similar to voting in that your vote counts. But it's not going to it's not going to be the biggest influence depending on how big the corporation is. If we own a lot of stock, if we own 51 percent, then we have complete influence in terms of what's going to happen. So again if you own something like a publicly traded stock like if you own a few stocks of Apple or Google then you're not going to have much influence although you still have the Voting.

In a similar fashion as when you vote for a representative your single vote probably isn't going to be that influential but still the populace has the power of that vote to vote for representatives who then make decisions including hiring management management and then acting as agents in order to hire other employees and run the business. So if you think about the hierarchy then you can have something like You know it's the stockholders then the Board of Directors and then you've got like the president and whatnot. And then the vice presidents here that we can break out and you can think of the whole corporate structure that we can have which will differ based on the type of industry that we have and how it's centralized versus decentralized we can have it.

But just note that the corporate structure is typically going to be a very structured type of corporate structure almost like a military type of structure that we're going to have here, the stockholders being the ultimate owners. But they hire the board of directors and then you're going to have the structure of the organization which could include top management such as the president and then the folks below them and then below them in terms of the hierarchy which again could be broken out in terms of a very centralized system or in terms of a more decentralized manner.

Stockholder rights the stockholder has a right to vote for on stockholder meetings these days and which is huge so that the stockholder has that ability. And when you think about being a closely held company or or a sole proprietor versus a publicly traded company or a corporation when you sell stock. Note that Of course you're giving someone not only an equity interest to earn some of the revenues in the company but also I say a vote in what's happening in the company so it's important to keep that in mind.

The right to sell stock. So again the corporate stock being something that's standardized allows us to be able to sell the stock in a much easier fashion than if we were say a partnership receiving dividends. Now I know that that's a So unlike a partnership where when you have a drawl of a partnership each individual owner can make draws in accordance with their capital account and the agreements of the partnership agreement with the dividends involved here because all the stock and all the corporate stock is the same. And one of the benefits and and and drawbacks is that you can't just be a corporate owner and draw out whatever you want no matter how many stocks you have because you did that the divisions need to be the same for all shares.

So if there's a decision to give dividends and you are an owner of the stock you are entitled to a dividend equivalent to however many stocks you have and the distribution. So again that's a benefit and can be kind of thought of as a drawback too. But that's part of the standardization of the corporate stock. So when this happens, when the stocks are leaving the company, when we are the company that makes a decision to give some of the earnings back to the investors, we do it in the terms of dividends instead of draws . And because all the stocks are the same, we have to give an equal dividend to all common stockholders. A stock certificate.

Now a lot of times the stock certificate is often something we might not physically have. You can take the stock certificate in our safe deposit box or something. But typically it's an electronic certificate but it's still going to be a share of stock as a unit of ownership and that's going to give us you know proof that's going to be the proof of ownership of a stock within a company. When looking at the financial statements the stockholders equity chapter is often one of the most confusing components we hear when we look at the component of the stockholders equity related to the common stock. One of the confusing components of it is that we'll have this kind of terminology that will be included often.

And this is a benefit but it can also be a little confusing to look at. It's part of the standardization that we have for a corporation member. Remember that if we're talking about a predator or partnership we're just going to try to track the capital accounts. How much is owed to individual owners when we go to a corporation. However we're not tracked by individual owners. We're not going to say this is Sam. This is Lisa's capital account. That's not what we have because what we have is a standardized set of shares that are out there doesn't really matter who even owns them.

On the financial statements we need to determine who owns them when we get the dividends and whatnot. But in terms of the financial statements we need to say this is how many shares are outstanding. This is how many shares are out there. They're all the same, all the shares are the same. They all have the same par value. Now this isn't the market value. This isn't what we actually sold them for. We're just going to give this arbitrary par value number that makes it easier for us to standardize the shares. And then we also list out the number of shares that we could issue. These are the number of shares authorized to issue. So in other words we can say this is basically saying that this company could issue 150000 shares. They have the legal right to do so. They have only issued and have outstanding 100000 shares.

And there's a par value of five dollars which is not the market value that's not what we sold it for. That's not how much you can buy shares for but it gives us standardization of the shares. In other words if I take this 500000 here and divide it by five that's how many shares are outstanding. So that kind of standardization is what that par value is for. This represents similar to the interest in the investment. How much or part of the investment that was put into the company as opposed to the accumulation of value of revenue minus the distribution which will be retained earnings. So note that the par value is not the same as the market value.

So when we see the common stock on the books, if there is a par value which a lot of times there will be an arbitrary number which seems unusual at first but it's there to give us a standardization component. We'll talk more about that arbitrary number and why it's not the market value, how it relates to the marquee value, how to record the issuance of stock when we will sell it for the market value when there's a par value in later chapters.

Multiple Choice Questions - Corporations

In this chapter we will take a look at multiple tours questions related to corporations. First question: number of shares a corporation can sell a issued stock B outstanding stock C common stock the preferred stock and the authorized stock. So we'll go through this again and see if we can eliminate some options with the process of elimination.

Question number of shares a corporation can sell an issued stock. So the stock that is issued. And again we're going to try to go through these and just see if we can eliminate some of those that would be more obviously not part of the problem in order to go through the process of elimination. Now the issue in stock may not be a term that we fully understand so we could keep that for now. They issued outstanding stock.

The number of shares a corporation can sell. So if they're outstanding in that you know that might tell us that they haven't been sold. They're outstanding; they're out in the market. So that really doesn't tell us just by the terminology. That's what could be sold basically by the terminology. Looks like what has been sold so I don't think that outstanding stock would be its common stock now the common stock is basically just a kind of stock it doesn't really tell us the number of the common stock which would typically be what we're talking about. That could be distributed so common stock doesn't really tell us how many shares could be distributed. DS says preferred stock. And again that's another kind of stock.

Typically we're talking about common stock when talking about numbers of shares distributed but preferred stock doesn't tell us the number of shares by that name. You would think that just telling us what type of stock we're talking about. So I'd say we can eliminate the and e says authorized stock. And that sounds like some kind of legal term that could give us some authorization for the issuance of stock so we're left with a and e Let's go through this again and wool's will pick the final answer. The number of shares a corporation can sell is either A or E either issued stock or authorized stock. So between those two Of course the issued stock would mean that we already sold them. They've been they've been or they're they're issue. So the authorized stock on the other hand is what we could issue what we could sell. So this is the authorized stock. In other words it is not what's outstanding there that's what could be outstanding.

Well we have the legal right to be outstanding at this point. Outstanding is what's actually in the market at this time. The correct answer is e.. So one last time. Number of shares a corporation can sell the authorized stock next question. Corporate board of directors aims are voted on by management to run the normal corporate activities see are the stockholders D. Are government agents and E have final authority for managing corporate activities. So we will go through this again with the process of elimination.

Corporate board of directors aims are voted on by management. So if we don't really understand the board of directors we might think maybe management votes for the board of directors. Maybe management is the one that does that so I'll keep that for now. DS says to run the normal core corporate activities. Now the board of directors doesn't normally run the corporate activity but is actually run by management. So the day to day meaning the day to day work is done by the employees. Employees including the upper management which would then hire employees to run the day to day operations. So I'd say the board of directors now does not really run the normal day-to -day stuff.

See are the stockholders and you might think that's I'll keep that for now. And Dee says our government agents now the board of directors doesn't necessarily need to be government agents so the government may regulate like the FCC Securities and Exchange Commission or whatnot but not really the board of directors. Those are not government agents. Hopefully. He says have final authority for managing corporate activities. And then seems like reasonable to note also when we look at these types of problems if there's one answer that seems more you know longer and more detailed Not that there's anyone that's too long here or too detailed I would say that you may want to give that one more consideration because oftentimes a longer more detailed answer is trying to hedge any type of wrong statement in it meaning it's trying to be as specific as possible in order to be correct.

So if there's a longer statement that seems more defined than that may be one that you would consider more so if we didn't know what the answer was. So if we go through this again corporate board of directors either a C or E M A are voted on by management. C are the stockholders and E have final authority for managing corporate managing corporate activities. So if we look at ANC votes, the management are the stockholders. If you look at those two you might start to think more who are the stockholders who are the board of directors who are management.

And when we start to piece this together the stockholders are the owners, most stockholders then are in ultimate control but they do so by voting on the board of directors and then the board the directors hires management. So it's not the case that management hires the board of directors or votes on the board of directors. The board of directors assigns management and the stockholders are the ones that are going to vote on the board of directors. So that means that the board of directors are not necessarily stockholders the stockholders are going to be the ones that determine who is on the board of directors and therefore will act as agents for the best interest of the stockholders and then essent have final authority for managing corporate activities and that's alternately the case So the day to day activities are going to be done by management and the board of directors has the final authority because they are the ones that are responsible for putting management in place and making those type of overarching decisions rather than a day to day decisions. So one more time corporate board of directors corporate board of directors have final authority for managing corporate activities.

Issuing Common Stock for Cash

Within the issue in common stock for cash chapter of the Book we will take a look at the transaction for the issuance of common stock for cash. This is often the initial type of transaction that's going to happen for a corporation. In other words the corporation will often issue stock in order to get that initial investment from the stockholders who are the owners and the shareholders of the corporation in order to finance future operations. The issue of common stock doesn't happen as much as we might think when we think of the stock market because we often think of stocks trading all the time which they do trade all the time.

But remember that when we're talking about publicly traded stocks trading on the Stock Exchange we're talking about stock that is mainly traded between two traders not from the issuance of the corporation the corporation typically issuing more rarely and in terms of having an initial offering and then other types of issuance throughout the time period. But most of the trading we see is going to be from traders within the stock market. The issuing of common stock is going to be similar. We can think of it as similar to a partnership or so prior to that, putting in that initial investment into the company in order to start the company.

We'll take a look at this in terms of our chapter chapter to go through the process and comp concepts. Then we'll take a look at it in terms of an excel sheet where we can work through the problem with a step by step instructional chapter. The actual

Excel sheets have one tab that will give the answer for it generally. And then another tab where we can walk through the process step by step along with instructional chapters. The Excel sheets will be pre-formatted so that we will learn some excel in terms of self relationships. But we won't need to format the cells. They will be pre-formatted so that we can work on the learning of the concepts.

Stock for Cash

In this chapter we will take a look at a journal entry for a transaction for a corporation issuing stock for cash. We're going to go through a scenario which will look like this. We have the information up top. We're going to record a journal entry for it in the general journal, then we'll post that to a trial balance so we can see a quick result of what will happen. So we're going to post it to this trial balance worksheet over here.

We are formatted in terms of cash. Our only assets are going to be a very small trial balance. But we want to see something in balance recorded see the effect on the accounting equation as well as individual accounts. We have assets and liabilities in one range. We have the equity lightly. Revenue and expenses. The dark blue the zero here represents that the positive numbers on this form of our debits the negative numbers are credits and therefore debits minus the credits equals zero debits therefore equal credits net income is zero because there is no revenue or expense on this current trial balance.

We're going to have a transaction of the issuing of stock so we're going to issue stock from the corporation. It's important first to note that this is different from trading stocks when we buy stock or when we sell stock particularly when we buy stock. It might be thought that we're buying that from the corporation. We're not typically if we buy stock such as Apple or Google. We are typically buying it from others who are just selling the stock. That's the beauty of stock. It's interchangeable when the corporation issues stock. They often do that on the initial offering. When we start the corporation because that will be a way to generate capital from investors or periodically from time to time later on in the process. But note that the issue in a stock isn't something that happens all the time. It's something that like when we start a business we issue stock in that.

And if we were to start a sole proprietor we would put our own capital into the business or a partnership would put their own money into the business for a corporation the stockholders put their own money into the business and they do so by buying stock. So it's the same kind of process there. What's happening is the owners and the stockholders are putting money into the business in order to have an equity interest in the business decision making interest within the business in a similar format as any type of business would.

When we start the business in order to get that initial investment to get the business going once we have that initial investment then hopefully my company makes money and we don't have a lot more investment from the owners but have payments from the owners from the company in the form of a corporation. Those would be dividends. So this is going to be us investing in the company. We're going to issue 20000 shares from the company.

We have a five dollar par value and we're going to issue them for $10. So remember the goal here is basically to get capital typically. So we're trying to generate revenue so we can have operational money to use later on within the business. So cash is going to be increasing. We issued 20000 shares. The tricky part here is that how much are we going to which one of these are we going to use the five dollar par or the $10 market price. Why are there two? Which one are we going to use when we sell the stock we're going to sell it for whatever the price is on the market. So just like anything we're going to get whatever we can for it. So the cash is going to go up with a debit cashing a debit balance account.

We're going to do the same thing to increase it with the debit. The calculation will be twenty thousand shares times the market price $10. And just remember when we're talking about cash the cash compartment of our selling of our stock we're going to get whatever we want. What can we afford on the market? This will almost always be the market price higher than the par value price. Then what's going to be the other side of this. Well if we were investing in a sole proprietor or a partnership the other side would be some type of capital account in the equity chapter. Same thing here it's going to be in the equity chapter but we're not going to call it a capital account because unlike a partnership we're not going to try to list all the owners of the corporation.

The beauty of a port corporation is that all of the shares are the same. The only difference between the owners is how many shares they own. So that's the great thing about it: it's all standardized. So we're not going to list out like people's names here of who we owe as we would with a partnership. What we're going to do instead is list out the common stock and then the retained earnings are the main two components. So the common stock represents us putting money into the business. The retained earnings represents the business cumulating revenue over the process of the business over and above the initial investment less anything that was given back out to the owners in the form of dividends which are similar to draws for a sole proprietor. So we're going to be up here.

We're working up here. Now we have these two things up here. This is confusing. We have the common stock with a par value and then we've got the paid in capital. Why do we have two things represented in the investment here? Well that's because the value is going to be a standardized number. This par value five dollars to five dollars is just an arbitrary number we like made up out of nowhere. Why would we make up a number? Because it's standardized. This number now is very standardized. This number represents how you know what it is: whatever is divided by 5 will be how many shares are outstanding. That's what the par value will do. It will make this very standardized.

What has this account been everything over and above what we got paid for the issuance of stock over and above the par value. This number will make no real sense over time because the market price will change and therefore there is no real relationship between the paid in capital and the number of shares outstanding because it just depends on when we issued the stock because the market price will change. But this one is very uniform because we're using a par value. So this one is going to have to go up. We're still going to credit equity just like we would for a sole proprietor or partnership but we're first going to credit the common stock par value and we're going to credit that for in this case a 100000.

How are we getting that? We're going to take the 20000 shares we issued times the par value $5. The smaller the number that's almost always going to be, it's pretty much always going to be smaller than the market price. So we're going to increase that by 100,000. And then the difference is going to go to paid in capital which is just the 200000 minus the 100000 or whatever we need the plug to make this in balance to make the credits equal to the debits. So this number is like we say it has no real uniformity.

Number numbers are just whatever we need to do in order to balance this thing out. If we post them, cash is going to go up. That's the point of issuing the stock. We're given an equity investment to some owners that basically have some owning potential, giving them some voting rights; they have the ability to influence the company in some ways and the right to receive dividends when they are declared in exchange for the cash. So cash is going up. And then we're going to record that we owe these people money not by name but by increasing the common stock that we issued. Five hundred thousand plus one hundred. Now it doesn't really matter for the corporation who owns it.

Well we'll determine that when we make the distributions in terms of dividends and whatnot. But as far as the financial statements go it doesn't matter. I don't need to we don't need to list who owns the stock. Whoever owns it it's fine. They're all the same. The stocks are all the same. So we're just going to say hey we issued 20000 more. It's increasing the Comstock by 100000 to 600000. And then we can just easily know how many shares are out there because we can say OK it's 600000 divided by the par value or five. There's 120000 shares out there. The financial statements again don't show us who owns them right now. You know the notes could tell us that but the financial statements themselves don't tell us who owns the shares but we know how many shares are out there.

And if we own any share they'll all be uniform in terms of our voting rights for each in particular share and for the amount of evidence that we're going to get and what we should get upon liquidation of the company then we're going to increase the paid in capital this 100000 increase in the 60. So the 60s went up by 100,000 to 160000. So here's our total transaction. This is what has been invested over life. This is what had been invested first. This is not the initial offer he made. Otherwise this would be you know these would be zero and it would go up so there and they would have already been stocks that were issued in the past.

We are increasing it here this account being very uniform because we're increasing it just by the par value times the number of shares and this one is a number that is going to be anything over and above that again in total. This just represents the investment by the owner's investment by stockholders as opposed to this number retained earnings which is going to represent the earnings that have been accumulated over and above the initial investment. It's important for a corporation to keep those separate because when we make distributions and things like that we don't want to take it out of the initial investment.

We want to take it out of our earnings. We want to pay people for the earnings we want to pay people at the performance of the corporation after the corporation earns revenue. We want to take those revenues and pay it out. We don't typically want to pay back the initial investment if we do it might be treated differently for things like taxes so if we go over here to the stockholders equity kind of chapter of the financial statements we can see the format that the stockholders equity will take. It's often a bit confusing to look at the stockholders equity chapter. It can be intimidating at first especially if we're dealing with a partnership that doesn't have a lot of partners or a sole proprietor where we only have one equity account.

Just remember when we're dealing with a corporation it's all the same like if we took this number in total. It's just the same thing. That's how much we owe if one person owned all of the stock from the corporation then in essence we would owe them 600,000 plus 160000 plus 658 thousand the one million four hundred eighteen thousand. So just like we would with a sole proprietor, the same as the assets one for three eight thousand minus twenty thousand will be that one for one for one eight thousand. So assets minus liabilities equals that total equity chapter. The only difference with the corporation is we're going to break it out by once again the initial investment the stock that was purchased versus the earnings of the life of the business in the equity chapter we're going to say this stockholders equity unlike a financial statement we're going to say this is the common stock we will list that it's a five dollar par value and we'll tell how many shares are out authorized this means how many shares.

Basically they're allowed legally to issue. They could issue 150 shares. However only 120000 shares are issued and outstanding which again we can clearly see on the financials if there's a par value by taking this number 600000 divided by the five dollars the 120 is the number of shares outstanding. So and then we and then we're going to have the amount 600000 then the paid in capital is the 160 all that represents is how much we got paid over and above the par value par value is just an arbitrary number.

The 600 plus the 160 or the 760 is what we actually get paid for selling our stock and then the retained earnings is going to be this component. And that's just going to be the amount of earnings that have accumulated over the life of the business less anything that's been taken out in the form of draws. The six seven sixty six fifty eight is the one million for 18 this represents the total value of equity if there's only one owner. It would be like we would owe that one stockholder the one million for 180000 misrepresenting.

In other words the book value of the company also represents assets minus liabilities in the same way as any type of instance he would a sole proprietor or a partnership would still the total capital is the total capital. In essence it's the book value of the company.

Worksheet - 20 Issuing Stock for Cash

In this chapter will record a transaction related to the issuance of common stock data that will be on the left side. We're going to enter that into the journal entry here, the general journal. We will post that not to the general ledger but to a worksheets so that we can see a really quick example of what the effect will be on the accounting equation as well as individual accounts.

We'll have the beginning worksheet here at the Beacon in balance the Indian balance the balance is in order as all trade balances all our assets and liabilities equity income and expenses assets and green liabilities and Orange the equity chapter in light blue revenue and expense income statement in dark blue which is going to give some accounts here so we can see the balancing process when we record this information. The most difficult part about corporate transactions is the equity chapter oftentimes because it's broken out a little bit different than we may see it for an individual it's basically broken out. In terms of the capital investments and then the retained earnings less has been earned over the life of the company less.

Any evidence that has been given out to owners. It's a little bit different than we might see in a partnership where we're going to just track things by what is owed to individual partners. So that's where we want to concentrate here at the standardization of Corporation stock and that's what we'll be working on here. Note that we have the debits are not bracketed the credits are bracketed. In other words excelsis debits have positive credits as negative and debits minus the credits then add up to zero. Therefore debits equal the credits. That's what the zero means net income is going to be revenue minus expenses. There are none on this trial balance. So we're going to issue stock here. So it says we're going to issue 20000 shares of $5 par value stock for $10.

It's important to note that a stock issued from the corporation's stock being bought from the corporation is much different than a normal stock sale, a normal stop transaction which is typically between two to stockholders. So whenever we see stock being bought and sold it's not typically being bought from the corporation it's being traded by two individuals owning stock. The beauty of stock is that it's all the same , it's all standardized. Therefore we can just treat it almost like currency, almost like coins. But the initial offering would be when the corporation initially sells their stock in order to generate capital in order to give some investment into the company and then they could issue stock at any other time throughout the business. But note that it's not something that's going to happen all the time.

It's going to happen when the company wants to generate capital through the issuance of stock; hopefully they issue stock at the beginning and then they generate revenue later. And rather than needing more capital by issuing more stock typically hopefully they're generating revenue and giving out dividends to the existing stockholders. So we're going to record this information here. We're going to say that they issued 20000 shares of $5 par a common stock. They're going to get it. First question is cash affected. We're going to say yes and that's generally the reason for the issuing of stock.

The company wants to generate capital to do what it needs to do. It needs to generate capital over and above or or the initial offering what they're receiving in revenue. So we're going to say cash is going to go into the business cash as a debit balance account. We're going to increase it by doing the same thing to it. Another debit so we're going to right click on f7 right click and copy it. I'm going to put it in the two in our journal entry right click and paste one two three just the values we could type in there as well. I like to copy and paste whenever possible.

Now the problem is that we sold 20000 shares but then it's got this five dollar power value and. And then we sold it for $10. What does that mean? In essence we have a value and a market value. The value really is just an arbitrary number. And this used to be really confusing to me. Still, you know it's a little weird to think about why we would just make up a number for the par value. And one reason is that it is going to be a way for us to standardize everything. So if I see something that's in the common stock here then I can standardize exactly how many stocks are there by using the par value and that's that standardization process is one of the core advantages to stock. So par value is just going to be an arbitrary kind of a placeholder, a number which helps us to standardize the stock. It's not what we actually got for it.

The price here that we sold it for $10 is the market price. And Of course we're selling stock. Our stock just like we would sell anything else looking for the highest price. So the par value will typically be low priced lower than what we expect to sell the stock for we will sell the stock for whatever we can highest price possible at the point of sale. So the sales price and the market price will change over time. The par value price will not that's the point of the par value. So the cash then Of course is going to be calculated based on the market price. So we're just going to take that number of shares which was 20000 times the market price. $10 dollars we're going to get two hundred thousand. We'll do that same calculation here in and. See 2 in Excel will see equals.

Will type in the 20000 times the $10 and enter. Okay. So then that's what we're going to get. We're going to issue the common stock now that's going to be in the equity chapter. Common stock is similar to the capital account for a sole proprietor or partnership. It represents what is owed to the owners to the stockholders. A little bit different however in that the common stock only represents what was invested. It doesn't represent as does the capital account for a partnership or a sole proprietor. What has accumulated over time in terms of revenue minus what has been taken out in terms of draws or dividends in a corporation we break out what has been invested in the common stock versus the accumulation of revenue over time the accumulation of earnings called retained earnings. So those two things are going to be broken out differently. That's the thing that's a bit different between the corporation's equity chapter and that of a sole proprietor, the equity chapter as a whole.

You can think of it as just the same as it all adds up to what is owed to the owners if you add it all up its assets minus liabilities. It's just that we need to break it out between the owners in a different way. Owners are all shareholders which are basically people holding tokens that are all worth the same amount of the company. If it's all common stock. OK. So we're going to say that the common stock is going to go up like the capital account. It has a credit balance. We're going to make it go up by doing the same thing to it's another credit. So we're going to.

Right click on Left-Hand right click and copy. We're going to put that in B-3 right click and paste one two three. Again you can type it in there if you so choose. We're going to go to the credit side this time. And now this is the tricky part. We're going to take the 20000 that is not going to be the 200000 that goes in there. In other words because there's a par value and that means that we want to standardize the common stock number. And so we're going to use the five dollar amount to do that. So we're going to take the 20 thousand times the five dollar par or one hundred thousand is how much the common stock is going up by. So I'm going to put in D-3 in which to do that same calculation but make it a negative by saying instead of equals negative twenty thousand times five 20000 times five negative 20000 times five that'll give us a negative or credit of 100000.

The difference then Of course is 200000 minus 100000 or 100000 that we need in order for the debits to equal the credits. I'm going to do that with our negative some formula plug formula which is negative as you double click the sum function and highlight those cells. So we're going to say the 200 minus the 100. We need another 100 to be in balance what will that go to. It's going to go to the additional paid in capital. And so these two accounts can be confusing when you first learn these two accounts. When we first learned these two accounts because you would think you would just go to the common stock but we have this par value and therefore that will standardize this amount.

Meaning this amount will always be in standard format. It'll always be in units of five dollar par value. So we can easily figure out how many stocks were traded by taking whatever is there divided by five dollars that will give us the amount of stocks that are issued and outstanding. But if not how much money we got for those stocks because that varies depending on when we sell the stock with the stock price. So the adding up of these two amounts the additional paid in capital what was paid over and above the par value for the stocks issued and this common stock number is what we actually received in investment for the issuance of our stock.

So in other words the paid in capital in excess of par for the common stock is just that it's what we got paid over and above the par value for the common stock we issued because Of course we're going to issue it at whatever market price is there and the par value is set at a standard price generally far below what we believe what the market price will be. So it's going to be a credit as well it's going to increase the equity chapter. So we're going to right click and copy. We're going to put that in before right click and paste one two three. So there's going to be our journal entry. Let's post it and see what happens. We're going to post cash.

First here is cash in the journal entry. Here it is on the balance. We want to be in H 7 where we will say equals point to that cash is going to bring the cash up by 200000. So here we got the cash going up by 200000 here then the common stock here it is in the journal entry. Here it is on the trial balance and we're going to be in H 10 and just say equals and point to that one hundred thousand bringing the 500,000 balance up. So there has already been common stock issued. We're issuing more at that time at this time to 600000 then the additional paid in capital at age 11. We're going to say equals and we're going to point to this one hundred thousand.

Second it's going to go from 60000 up by 100000 to 160000 and that will then put us back in balance here and there we have it cash went up. But there's no effect on net income, no effect on the revenue or expenses. We got cash from operations not from doing work but from issuing stock to stockholders. That's one of the major benefits of a corporation. We can generate capital by giving equity investment by issuing stock to stockholders increasing our cash here even though we haven't generate any revenue. So that's what we have and the revenue increases or the capital revenue does not increase the capital increases here.

And so no the breakout here was increasing in this case part of total equity which is all this total equity is 1 million for 18000 which equals revenue minus expenses just like with a sole proprietorship or partnership the total equity represents what is owed to the owners. We don't need to break out individual owners as we do with a partnership because they all own the same shares meaning every share an individual owner could own more shares but all shares are the same for common stock shares. So all an individual can do is own more or less shares and it's not like each share has a different type of rights or or type of piece of the company or ownership of the company as is the case with the capital account for a partnership.

Therefore what we're going to do is we're just going to break out instead of each individual share each individual owner as we do with the partnership. We're going to break out the amount that was invested in the partnership versus the accumulated earnings of the partnership less anything that we gave out in terms of dividends. And that's how we'll break out the equity chapter here. So if we look at this in terms of the stockholders equity the most confusing question is if we just look at the stockholders equity chapter of say it like a financial statement the most confusing component is really just the wording in the timing of it.

And so the stockholders equity has common stock and we're really going to generally see the par value that will be written in here the par value in this case being five dollar par value and then it'll have the amount that will be authorized 150 shares authorized That's how many they could legally give away. So choose and give or sell if they so choose. And then we're going to have the amount that were actually issued that they chose to issue these amount of shares and that's when we can actually find if there's a par value by looking at the financials saying OK there's six hundred thousand common stock 600000 common stock divided by the par value of five dollars that means 120 shares must be out there because the par value is the same for all shares unlike the market value which changes over time. So we could say OK there's 120 shares thousand shares out there.

So then we can just bring these numbers over in terms of our numbers here where we can say OK the amount issued in outstanding is going to be this 600000 so and I'm going to put it in AM 10. I want to flip the sign so I'm going to put a negative on that number and that's how much is outstanding. Then we've got the payment in capital which again I don't want to credit over here so it's going to take that number and flip the sign by saying instead of equals negative of that number. And that's the amount that was invested. I'm going to go ahead and put some of them up on the right hand side so we can see that Capital Investment equals some in an 11 double click the SUM function and highlight those two numbers 600 plus 160 is 760.

And then we're just going to take the retained earnings which is the accumulation of revenue. And no we didn't do anything with retained earnings. When will it be affected when we close out retained earnings to when we close out the net income these accounts down here to retained earnings in the closing process. So within retained earnings I'm going to say a negative of this number and enter and that means that the total stockholder's equity what is owed to the owners and again I would think about it as this way as if as if only one would have one individual owned all the stock that would be basically this number here just like a sole proprietor. What if it was a sole proprietor or completely owned corporation by one individual that would be the sum of these two equals the sum.

Doubleclick the sum of the 760 and the 6:58. And I'm going make this a little bigger one million for 18. And that Of course is the revenue mine or the assets minus the liabilities also equaling $1 in 418. So this is what is actually owned by or owed to the owners. It's going to be broken out by owners in terms of stockholders because all the stockholders are all the same or all the stocks are all the same. And the only thing that differs is how many stocks we own. We don't have to break out the owners by name or by how much is owed to any particular owner as we deal with a partnership. We can just have it all be the same. It's just like tokens on a stock and therefore breaks it out in terms of to give us a little bit more detail.

What has been invested in capital investments versus debt earnings. And another reason that's really important is because when we distribute the earnings of a corporation they're often taxable. So when we give the earnings back to the corporation, if we make money then give the money back to the individuals who had invested in the corporation in the form of dividends; those dividends, unlike draws, are typically taxable. And it's important for us to know whether the divisions we give are going to be from earnings which means they are taxable.

Typically if we give back the original investment then that's not really earnings and it shouldn't. You would think from a logical standpoint we won't get into tax law here but it shouldn't be really taxed out if we're just if they invested money and we're just giving it back we didn't make any money. There's no earnings and we gave it back. It shouldn't be taxable so for a few different reasons we need to break out the retained earnings. It will give us a sense of what has been earned versus what has been just invested through its owners through the purchase of stock.

Multiple Choice Questions - Corporations

In this chapter we will take a look at multiple choice questions related to corporations. First question. Primary class of stock a preferred stock the normal stock see common stock the standard stock and e stock. So let's go through this again. We're going to say use the process of elimination and see if we can eliminate some of these options and narrow them down. Primary class of stock is a preferred stock. So the primary class where I'm thinking about the question is trying to ask what's the most you know about normal shares of stock. What's that? If we buy stock in a corporation what are the primary stockholders shares preferred stock.

If not them that's going to be a preferred or kind of a special stock or a different stock. It's not really preferred No it's preferred in terms of it gets paid dividends before other stocks but it has benefits and negatives to other types of stocks so it's not preferred stock normal stock. Well that seems kind of like it might be a normal stock so I'll keep that for now. Common stock now that one probably rings a bell. We might hear about common stock. That kind of rings a bell. The D says standard stock which sounds nice because it has two s's in it and whatnot but I don't think that's a thing. I don't think there's a standard stock I'm going to for now. And then he says stock and that doesn't really expand on what type of stock so as just a normal stock so I'm going to say that's probably not it. So we're between B and C.

We'll go through this again. Primary class of stock is either B or C either a normal stock or a common stock and between those two common stock is probably the one that sounds more familiar because that's the most common form of stock. So the prime last last run here is the primary class of stock is C common stock. Next question stockholders equity includes a time fixed assets paid in capital and retained earnings. See unearned revenue, the current assets and e discounts will go through this again and see if we can use the process of elimination to narrow this down. Stockholders equity includes fixed assets. Now the equity chapter is another account equation as its liabilities and equity and so if the term has assets it's probably not part of the equity chapter most likely. So it's not going to be a it's not going to be any kind of asset whether it be fixed current or non-current. So B says paid in capital and retained earnings for a corporation we may not know what paid in capital is or retained earnings but we probably recognize retained earnings as part of the equity chapter. So I'm going to keep that for now.

I see an earned revenue now that could be confusing because we have the term revenue in it and we know that revenue is kind of an income statement account but other than revenue is actually a liability account. You know we got paid and we didn't yet do the work. And so our liabilities aren't going to be in the equity chapter. So then DS says current assets and again it's an asset not an equity thing it says asset in the name so it's not that and then says discounts and discounts is generally on. It could be on the income statement as a contra revenue account, a sales discount at least. So possibly you know we can think of that as part of the equity in a way because it closes out the net income and that income is part of equity.

I want to keep the and e and go through this again. Stockholders equity includes either B or E either paid in capital and retained earnings or e discounts. So of those two I would think that retained earnings is most familiar because that's clearly in the equity chapter. And then it's between paid and capital and discounts and between those two paid in capitals is actually in the equity chapter whereas discounts is kind of part of net income which would roll into our retained earnings. So that would be I guess less correct most correct would be the B as the correct answer. Last time stockholder's equity includes being paid in capital and retained earnings.

Issuing Common Stock for Non-Cash

Within the issue in common stock for the non-cash chapter of the Book will go through the journal entry for the issuing of Comstock for a corporation. But this time not for the normal type of cash transaction. In other words, given common stock for the equity investment for these stock investments from the owner of the stockholder in exchange for cash. But this time in exchange for something other than cash.

And remember that although cash is going to be the most type most common type of exchange for something like stock and most things it will it's not the only thing that can be given anything of value can be given to the company in exchange for the stocks for example equipment could be given to the company in exchange for a stock purchase. We'll take a look at this.

In terms of a chapter to go through the concepts We'll take a look at this in terms of an excel worksheet which will have an answer tab. You can see how it all works together and fits together. Then we'll have a excel sheet that will have a pre-formatted excel sheet that can work along with an instructional chapter step by step in order to apply the concepts we have learned.

Issuing Stock for Non-Cash Asset

In this chapter we will record a transaction for the issue of stock for a non-cash asset. So in other words we're going to issue stock but not for cash we're going to get something else we're going to get equipment the information for this transaction will be on the upper left. We're going to record this to the general journal here and then we will post it not to the general ledger but to a worksheet to give us a quick example of the effect on the accounting equation and individual accounts our trial balances in order by ask that same drain liabilities in orange equity and light blue and income and expenses the income statement dark blue debits are non bracketed credits are bracketed the debits minus the credits are represented by this green zero meaning that the debits do indeed equal the credits no net income at this time. That means that the revenue and expense accounts are all zero.

So this is just a quick trouble to show us something that is in balance which is really useful and important when we record these transactions so we can get an idea of the double entry accounting system. And what's the effect on the different accounts and the accounting equation? What we're going to do here is issue stocks as we did in a prior chapter but this time rather than getting cash we're getting something else we're getting equipment. So it is entirely possible it is just like any type of transaction we have here typically we transact for cash but very possible to transact for something else as well.

In this case we're going to issue ownership in the company which is going to be giving stock which is going to provide some type of ownership, some type of voting potential rights to the people purchasing stock in exchange for something of value. That being the equipment. So we're going to have the issuance of 20000 shares of five dollar par value stock for equipment valued at 150000. So first we get. We usually think about what we're going to get if we're not getting cash. We're going to get equipment so we can put the equipment on the books. Equipment is an asset. That's what we're getting.

Assets have debit balances we're going to make it go up by doing the same thing with another debit. So Will debit the equipment now. Note that many problems will just give us the equipment value. It's important to note that we're basically doing a kind of a market exchange here. We're selling our stock for the equipment. So we're going to have to agree upon the value of the equipment and the stock we might use either one of those things to value the other. In other words if the equipment has a stated value or market value we know that equipment is selling for 150 thousand we might use that then to determine what the market price of the stock is. If on the other hand were sent to stock is very standard like it's on a public exchange. Then we have a pretty good idea what this stock market price is because it's selling for that market price.

We may use that for us to figure out what the equipment value is. So we're kind of doing a market transaction here and we'd have to do some idea about what the correct market price for the equipment is. If it's kind of unique equipment then it might be a little bit more difficult to figure out that market price. If it's equipment that's being sold all the time and it's new then it might be pretty easy to figure it out. The stocks are the same way as the actual market price of the stocks. If it's a privately held corporation you may not know it because we don't really sell the stocks all the time. We don't know exactly what the stock is worth and if on the other hand we'd have to appraise it possibly or something. If on the other hand it's trading on a stock exchange then we know pretty well we have a pretty good idea of what the stock is worth that time because they're all the same. That's the beauty of stock if they're trading for a particular price at any given time that's pretty much what they're worth at that given time. So we're going to say the equipment's going to go up. Then we're going to credit something now just like if we were to invest like in a partnership or sole proprietor.

We know that we would invest in this case. And then the other side would go to the capital account for an owner. In this case we're not going to list out the owners. We don't need to list out the owners. That's the beauty of a corporation. The only way the owners are represented is that they are holding shares of stock. And however many shares of stock they hold. That's the differentiation between the owners that can hold more or less stocks in relation to other owners. So all we need to do then is credit here still. But we're going to credit the common stock account representing the fact that there's more stock out there.

We're going to do that first at the port of value. So we're going to credit the par value that will make things standardized. How do we do that? We're going to take the 20000 shares times the par value $5 increase, increasing it by one hundred thousand. So it's a credit balance account. We're going to increase it by 100000 in the credit direction. Remember that this par value makes this standardized, it's making this number a very uniform standardized number. That's the nice thing about it. That's why using the par value is relevant; the par value number itself has absolutely no meaning.

Completely arbitrary in its form, its function is to standardize this number to make it uniform. Everything else is just going to go into the additional pain and capital the amount that is not uniform and it will have no tie out to the number of shares that are outstanding for the company because it depends on the market price the market price will differ. The market price here is being determined. You were negotiating it by the agreement here between the equipment we are getting and the value of the stock. So here we are saying the equipment's worth 150 the par value is 100. Therefore we need 50000 to go into the additional paid in capital in order for the credits to be equivalent to the 150 debit. If we post this out then we see the equipment we're posting here goes from 0 up by 150 to 150. Then we're going to post the common stock. It's going to go from 500000 up by 100000 to 600000.

Again note the uniformity here. This is the point of the par value. This is the point of the par value: sort of the six hundred thousand divided by five will tell us exactly how many shares are out there. That's why that nice math is why we have that. And then we've got the paid in capital at 50 it started at 60000 and goes up by 50 to 110000. This is where the sloppy part happens. We don't know. This means nothing. We can't nicely divide it out by a par value figure out the number of shares. We can't divide it by the number of shares and figure out the price we were paid all the time because the price we will pay will differ depending on when we sold it because the market price will differ as time passes. So here's what we got then.

The equipment is going up. The common stock is going up and the paid in capital is going up. This then is the part of the equity chapter that just represents the investment by the owners. Note there's no effect on net income here. We got something that had no effect on net income. Instead we owe money back to the owners. We're not going to list who paid it's who we owe the money to. We know who they are by the fact that they're holding shares and that's who we're going to end up paying when we pay out things like dividends or if we were to liquidate the company the earnings side of the equity chapter is here. So this represents earnings over the life of the company retained earnings does less any distributions we made in the format here of dividends.

Whereas if it was if it was a sole proprietor we would pay out stuff in the form of draws so here's just the stockholders equity chapter so we can get an idea of this and just see this long wording can be intimidating. Again the format of this can be intimidating because we're not just listing our capital accounts which can be pretty straightforward and just say hey we owe this much money to this partner or this much money to the owner with one capital account for a partnership or sole proprietor. Here we've got this longer setup but remember the whole thing is the same in total.

Meaning this whole blue accounted for if there's only one shareholder that owned all the shares then we would have the six hundred thousand plus the 110 thousand plus the six fifty eight thousand we would owe that one owner one million three hundred sixty eight thousand and that is represented in the book value of the company or assets one. What happened here. Assets of 1 2 3 8 0 0 0 8 million 1 million 238 Plus the 150 debits minus the credit or liability which will give us that 1 million 368 thousand. So this is the book value of the company. If we see that in terms of the statement of stockholder equity we typically write this whole thing out we say common stock has a five dollar should be you know it but $5 par value that's what the par value is an arbitrary number.

We could say there's one hundred fifty thousand shares authorized that means that we have the legal right to issue that many shares. Doesn't mean that that many shares have been issued and then we have to 120 shares issued and outstanding which we should be able to easily verify with this number coming in from here which is the six hundred thousand divided by five par 120. Then we've got the paid in capital paid in capital just representing what we got paid over the par value therefore the 710 the 600 plus the 110 represents the amount that we got in total investment for the selling of stock then the retained earnings.

Represents the amount that has been accumulated over time the retained earnings is where we're going to close out the closing process and close out net income to retained earnings. We keep those separate because when we pay dividends we want to pay them out of retained earnings. We don't want to pay them out of the initial investment that could have different consequences including tax consequences. We want to say hey we earned the money we're going to pay back that earnings to the investors and not touched. Typically that initial investment that's what we would like to have happen. So then there's total here representing the total stockholders the equity.

Worksheet - 30 Issuing Stock for Non Cash Assets

In this chapter we will record the journal entry to issue common stock when cash is not received we're going to issue the common stock and receive equipment instead. So issues in common stock for non-cash assets will be on the left side. We're going to record the journal entry here in the general journal, then we'll post it not to the general ledger but to a worksheet. Here's our beginning balance. This is where we will post that years are ending balance.

This will give us a quick look at the effects on the accounts as well as the effect on the accounting equation. We've got to ask that same dream we got the liabilities and owns the equity and the light blue the revenue and expenses in dark blue we can see that we're in balance because the the debits are non bracketed or positive for Excel and bracketed or credited for Excel or credits debits minus the credits equals zero. That's what the green zero indicates no net income is shown here at this time. This is just going to be a very you know short trial balance to give us an idea of something in balance so that we can see the effect it really is helpful for us to see a balancing mechanism and actually post these journal entries to something to a trial balance so we can see the effect on it and the effect on the accounting equation.

We Of course are going to be focusing here on the equity chapter for a corporation that's what typically differs for a corporation. And that will be broken out in terms of we're looking at common stock paid in capital for common stock. And then the retained earnings are not what we're focusing on here but noting that retained earnings is the accumulation of the revenue less any distributions to the owners dividends and the common stock represents how much the owners have invested in terms of capital investment. Okay so we're going to go over here we're going to say that there's 20 issue 20000 shares of $5 par stock for equipment valued at 150. So this is similar to just if someone wanted to buy into the corporation, remember this is different from trading because we're not buying from another individual like a stock trade typically would be.

We're buying stock from the corporation and rather than giving the corporation cash for that stock we're just giving something else of value in this case equipment. So to do that we need to kind of know the value of the equipment that was what they were giving. So that will determine basically the market price of the stock and that's really the confusing component here. And it may actually work the other way around. We might know the market price of the stock because of changing exchanges possibly on a market exchange and therefore the negotiation process might tell us basically what the equipment cost is.

But in any case there's a market transaction happening here and therefore it's going to determine the market transaction will determine or tell us what the prices of the equipment and or the market price of the stock that will differ than from the par value par value just being an arbitrary number that we assign to the stocks in order to standardize them. So to record this first we're going to say well is cash affected. And the answer for the corporation. No we didn't get cash, we sold it for equipment. So what did happen is that we got another asset we got equipment. What did we get?

Equipment equipment is also an asset. It's got a debit balance we need to go up. So we're going to do the same thing to it. Another debit. So I'm going to copy the equipment in f 8 right click and copy. We'll put that up top in the top right click and paste one to three just the values we could type in there as well. If we so choose, the amounts are just going to be the market value of the equipment. So they're going to typically give that in a problem we'd have to figure out what that would be in practice. And if our stock is traded on the exchange then whatever we determine that might help us to determine the market price of the equipment. So we're going to say the equipment is worth one hundred fifty thousand.

Then we're going to credit something. Now we're going to credit something in the capital chapter as we would just if we invested the equipment in a sole proprietor or a partnership. But this time we're going to issue stocks. So it's going to be some type of stock issuance that is going to be given for that equipment that's going to be the common stock. So it's a credit balance representing what is owed to the owners. We're going to make it go up by doing the same thing to it's another credit. So when I right click on the common stock right click and copy put that in the right click and paste one to three. Or we can just type it in there.

The tricky thing is that it's not going to be a credit for 150000. Why? Because there's a power of value and the par value is just going to be a standardized value. So it's not going to change with the market price. When we sell the stock we're going to sell it for whatever we can and therefore we're going to use whatever equipment that we can get. We're going to sell it for that because that's what we do at the market price. The par value will just give us a standard number so that it will standardize this number. So all we're going to do on the par value is take the 20000 shares we issued times 5 and that will be the one hundred thousand. So I'm going to do that with a calculation here by saying rather than equals negative twenty thousand times five.

And that will be the negative one hundred thousand. The difference between a hundred and fifty. We got in value for the equipment and the 100000 is 50000. What we need as a credit here in order to be in balance I'm going to do that with our negative sum function which is deployed formula negative as you Doubleclick the sum function highlight the 152 the one hundred and that'll give us the 50000 as a negative the one hundred and fifty. Now Of course equal in the 150 debit what accounts should go to additional paid in capital so members remember that these two represent what has been given to the company. So in terms of a capital investment, that's different. We're going to break that out differently here.

Unlike we do in a partnership or sole proprietor to what has been earned less what has been distributed in terms of dividends. So the retained earnings is what still remains in terms of earnings over and above what was initially invested. These two common stock additional paid and capital represent what was additional what was initially invested. Why do we need two accounts to give that because the par value will standardize those common stocks so that we can know exactly from this number how many stocks were issued by dividing it by the power value and the additional pay and capital will just represent whatever was paid over and above that par value because that will change with the market price as the market price changes. So this is going to go up.

It has a credit balance going to do the same thing to another credit we're going to copy this, sell this and have 12 right clicks and copies. We're going to put that in before right click and paste one two three. There's going to be our journal entry. Let's post this out now so here's the equipment account on our journal entry. Here it is on the trial balance. We're going to be here in age 8 where we will say equals point to that 150000 bring in the zero balance by 150 to 150. Here's the common stock we're going to be down here on common stock. Something's in it already. This is not the initial stock offering. We're issuing more stock at some point in the future from the initial stock offering. We're going to say equals and point to that one hundred thousand.

Bringing the 500000 up by 100000 to 600000. Then we're going to go to the paid in capital right underneath. Here's the Peyton cafe on the journal entry. Here it is on the trap balance. We're here in age 12 where we will say equals to that 50000 bringing the 60 up by 50 to 110. Note that the equipment went up. No effect on net income however. Even though we got something of value we got equipment. We think the company did not earn any revenue to get that equipment. What they did is give out some capital and some earning potential in that company. And so that's what. So that the ownership went up or the amount that's owed back to the owners in essence went up.

Okay so that's going to be our transaction we're going to go then over here and take a look at just the equity chapter of the calculation of equity in like more of a financial statement format where we would see this kind of confusing component in terms of the wording we'd have to say that the common stock. There's five dollar par common stock. This is the amount that was authorized. Meaning they have the ability to issue up to 150000 shares and how many are issued and outstanding. We could find that by looking at our numbers here and say well there's six hundred dollars worth of common stock divided by the power value which is five dollars.

I mean it's 120,000 issued outstanding. So that's kind of what's useful about that kind of symmetry. One hundred and twenty thousand. And then if we go over here we're going to put it in in 10 we're going to take this amount put it in 10. So that's going to be I don't want to, I don't want to credit. We wanted to make it positive. When I say negative of that number and enter and then we're going to do the additional payment in capital. We're going to put that here in 11 once again rather than equals negative of that number and enter going to some of them up on the right side in an 11 by saying equals as you double click the sum function. Highlight the 600 and the 110 or 7. Then we'll just pull over the retained earnings which we're not really dealing with in this problem. They would be affected by the accumulation of net income or close a net income out to retained earnings.

So we're going to say negative of this number and then if we sum this up it will be the sum of these two we're just adding these two of seven 710 plus 650 fifty eight that will be the total there I'm going to fix this real quick so Ken equation works at top. OK. So there is that. And so this is going to be our equity chapter. This is what would be over it too if it was just one owner. You can think of that if it was all the corporation was owned by one person who owned all the corporate stock then this would kind of be like a net value. In other words it equals the assets minus the liabilities one knowing three sixty thousand. How do we know who to pay that too?

We know who to pay that to just buy how many shares they have because all the shares are equal meaning if we liquidated the company and sold the equipment to pay off the liabilities we would have one million 6:38 if we sold for that would be the book value if everything worked out perfectly. And then we could just pay that in accordance with the shares. Basically because all the shares if there's only common stock shares are all the same. It's just the beauty of the corporation versus a partnership where Of course we have to track each individual partner's capital account because how much will be owed to the partners will differ.

And the only way we know that is by tracking their capital account with a corporation how much is owed to the owners will differ. But the way we know that is that they just own more or less stock which is just like kind of owning more or less dollars. They're all standardized units. So that's going to be one of the principal differences in the equity chapter between a corporation and something like a sole proprietorship or partnership.

Multiple Choice Questions - Corporations

This chapter we will take a look at multiple choice questions related to corporations. First question Pora values a common stock issued at low price the amount assigned by corporate charter the market value of stock. C D price stock is sold at or e priced used to calculate dividends. So we will go through this again and use the process of elimination and see if we can narrow this down to par value of a common stock issued at a low price. So par values common stock issue that low price. If it was issued at par value.

Possibly but it doesn't sound I'm going to say that's not it's not it's not a common stock issued at a low price par value b amount assigned by corporate charter. That sounds kind of reasonable. Possibly we don't know what par value is we can say maybe say market value of stock. And again we might say maybe par value market value. Maybe those are the same thing. DS says price stock is sold at. And again we might say. I don't really know. Maybe D and then e says Price used to calculate dividends and that one seems kind of unusual.

Why would we use a price to calculate dividends? I mean the board of directors would have to come up with dividends that are going to be paid somehow. Maybe they are going to use a par value but not necessarily. So I'm going to say. Doesn't look right I'm going to be left with B C and D. Let's go through this again. Power value either A B C or D either amount assigned by a corporate charter or market value of stock or price stock is sold at.

Now of those three we say par value and market value probably aren't the same thing. Market value of stock is not going to be the same exact thing as par value unless they're, you know, just two words for the exact same thing. So market values don't look like it's probably going to be it. Price stock is sold at or amount assigned by corporate charter. And again price stock is sold at probably the same thing as market value. That's what we're going to sell the stock for whenever we can get it. So C and D are kind of the same thing. Cs Ds basically defining c can't be both of them. So I'm going across those out and be left with B which is the amount assigned by corporate charter which is what the par value is. So the answer is B and just so we know the Parva is just an arbitrary number and that's going to be the amount assigned.

And the reason is just to have conformity with common stocks so it can be all standardized. So the final answer is the amount assigned by corporate charter. Next question amount received from stockholders in exchange for its stock over the par value is posted to a common stock, the preferred stock. See gain on sale of stock. The additional paid in capital E stock is always issued at the par value. Let's go through this again with the process of elimination of an amount received from its stockholders in exchange for its stock over the par value being posted to. So if we can break that down if we think about it we're saying OK we're receiving something from the stockholders in exchange for stock. So we're selling the stock and we got money over the par value.

We got something over the par value whatever that means. So if we don't know what that means we'll go through a process of elimination now of common stock which is kind of what they bought. They bought common stock. That's typically so we might say a maybe B says preferred stock. Now typically when we buy stock we're referring to common stock unless stated otherwise. So it's probably not a preferred stock. I'm going to say that's doesn't sound like C says gain on sale of stock which sounds kind of reasonable because we get there saying that we got more money than the par value of the stock. So maybe the stock is somehow worth the par value and we had a gain on the sale of stock. So I'm going to keep that for now.

D says additional paid in capital and again that might sound familiar as something that's just like in the equity chapter of the stock equity you don't know what it is. So it might go from that. I'll keep that for an hour. Sounds familiar and Isa's stock is always issued at the par value and that doesn't seem reasonable. Why would we always issue the stock at a set price? We're going to issue it whatever we can get for it. It's just like any other type of sale of something. We're going to get as much as we can eat so we're left with AC and Dean. Let's go through this again with amounts received from stockholders in exchange for its stock over the power value it is posted to.

We're left with a C or D either common stock or gain on sale of stock or additional paid in capital. So we've got an amount received from it shot in from stockholders in exchange for stocks and we did sell stock and we sold the common stock. But the common stock is going to be recorded at par value. So what we're really saying is we got paid something over par value. So it's not going to be the common stock as it were going to record the common stock at par value if you think of the journal entry we would we would get cash Might be good to write down the journal entry we would get cash let's say 100 dollars and then the par value would go to the common stock credited let's say $90 and we got more cash than the par value of let's say $10. Then the question is: Where does that go to again or does that go to additional paid in capital.

Now it's not a gain because we're not selling something you know of operations in the partnership we're still in the corporation, we're selling the corporation itself. We're selling equity interest in the corporation, not something like an asset in the corporation. So that means that it's not a gain from selling something that the corporation owns, we're selling the corporate component of the corporation. So it's going to be something in equity and that's something that's called additional paid in capital. So the final answer amount received from stockholders in exchange for its stock over the par value is posted to the additional paid in capital.